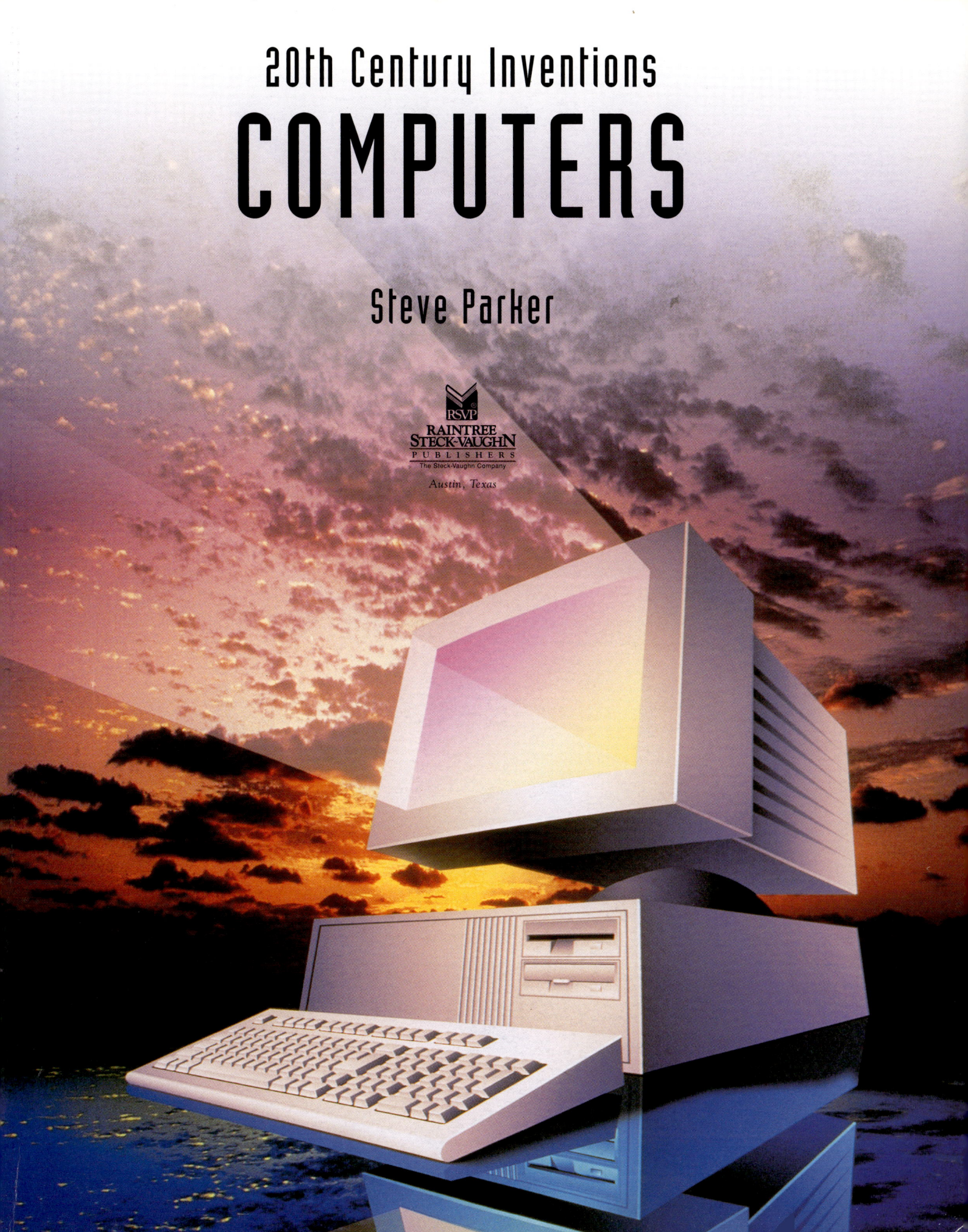

20th Century Inventions

COMPUTERS
LASERS
SATELLITES
TELECOMMUNICATIONS

Cover and title page: Computers are an important part of everyday life, offering exciting paths to knowledge and new ways of living.

© Copyright 1997, text, Steck-Vaughn Company

All rights reserved. No part of this book may be reproduced or utilized in any form or by any means, electronic or mechanical, including photocopying, recording, or by any information storage and retrieval system, without permission in writing from the Publisher. Inquiries should be addressed to: Copyright Permissions, Steck-Vaughn Company, P.O. Box 26015, Austin, TX 78755.

Published by Raintree Steck-Vaughn Publishers, an imprint of Steck-Vaughn Company

Library of Congress Cataloging-in-Publication Data
Parker, Steve.
Computers / Steve Parker.
    p.   cm.—(20th Century Inventions)
    Includes bibliographical references and index.
    Summary: Describes the development of computers, their various components, and uses for entertainment, education, business, and other facets of life.
    ISBN 0-8172-4811-0
    1. Computers—History—Juvenile literature.
    [1. Computers.]
    I. Title. II. Series.
    QA76.52.P37 1997
    004—dc20   96-31189

Printed in Italy. Bound in the United States.
1 2 3 4 5 6 7 8 9 0 01 00 99 98 97

Picture acknowledgments
Apple 27; Walt Disney 23; Eye Ubiquitous 5 (top)/Paul Seheult, 32/Kevin Wilton; Ronald Grant Archive 22/Walt Disney/Hollywood Pictures; Science Photo Library 7 (top), 9 (bottom)/Lawrence Migdale, 14/Astrid and Hans Frieder Michler, 15/Chris Gardner, 16/Dr. Jeremy Burgess, 24/Francoise Sauze, 25 (top)/Peter Menzel, 26/David Parker, 28 (top)/James King Holmes, 29/Hank Morgan, 30/Gregory MacNichol, 39 (bottom)/Damien Lovegrove, 42/Jerry Mason, 43 (top)/Philippe Plailly; Tony Stone Worldwide 4/Bob Krist, 5 (bottom)/Alan Levenson, 10/Zigy Kaluzny, 12/David Chambers, 20/Arthur Tilley, 21/Greg Pease, 28 (bottom)/Mark Wagner, 31/Michael Rosenfeld, 33/Andrew Sacks, 34/Chuck Keeler, 35/David Joel, 37 (top)/Charles Thatcher, 37 (bottom)/Michael Rosenfelf, 39 (top)/Michael Rosenfeld, 40/Jim Cambon, 43/Arthur Tilley; Telegraph Colour Library *cover, title page*; Topham 25 (bottom)/Associated Press; ZEFA 9 (top)/R. Du Buisson, 18, 36/B. Harrington III, 38, 45 (top)/R. Du Buisson. Artwork by Tim Benké, Top Draw (Tableau). All other pictures Wayland Picture Library.

CONTENTS

INTRODUCTION	4
THE FIRST COMPUTERS	6
HOW COMPUTERS WORK	10
GAMES AND ENTERTAINMENT	20
EDUCATION AND TRAINING	26
ART AND DESIGN	30
THE WORKPLACE	34
COMPUTER CRIME	40
THE FUTURE FOR COMPUTERS	42
DATE CHART	44
GLOSSARY	46
FIND OUT MORE	47
INDEX	48

INTRODUCTION

The control center's maps, charts, and graphs are generated and updated by computers, shown on computer monitor screens, and altered by pressing computer keys. In today's industrial and commercial world, few jobs are computer-free.

Have you used a computer today? You may not have actually sat down at a keyboard and screen, but the chances are you have benefited in some way from a computer. Dozens of the activities that make up daily life depend on computers, from the weather forecast and the school class schedule to home computer games and movie special effects. In every kind of business and industry, computers are vital tools.

Behind the scenes

Many of the computers used in offices, banks, and factories are largely automatic. For some of the time, they work by themselves, without any need for humans. They are linked to one another by telephone wires, fiber-optic cables in the telecommunications network, radio beams, satellites, and other marvels of modern technology. They "talk" to one another by electrical signals. But they are controlled by people.

A society built around computers

In the richer nations of the world, almost everyone has seen a computer. Many people have used one "hands-on." Computers are used for both work and play. Millions of people use them all the time in their jobs. In large organizations, whole departments are built around computers. Millions of other people use computers for leisure, pleasure, and entertainment, including computer toys and games. In recent years, more people are using computers for learning and education, and nearly every school has at least one.

Only a handful of scientific inventions have truly changed or revolutionized everyday life. They include the car, the television—and the computer. The pace of change is getting faster too. Some experts say that the revolution brought about by the computer has only just begun.

Computerized desktop publishing has condensed a roomful of people and equipment, from journalists to typesetters to photograph retouchers, into one small computer system.

The laptop computer goes anywhere, for use at any time—even on the beach! If a good idea suddenly strikes, it can be keyed directly into the machine.

What is a computer?

The name "computer" comes from the word "compute," which means to handle and process numbers, as in adding a sum. A computer is an electronic device that figures out answers according to a set of instructions called a program. Most computers do this much faster than the human brain. A computer also has a memory that stores numbers, words, and other information, known as data. As this book shows, there are many different kinds of computers.

THE FIRST COMPUTERS

Above Blaise Pascal's simple computing machine could add and subtract. Pascal (1623–62) invented it to help his father with his merchant business. The first commercial versions went on sale in 1645.

Mechanical "computers"

The first practical mechanical calculator—a machine with gears and levers for adding figures—was invented in 1642 by French mathematician Blaise Pascal. To use the calculator, he entered two numbers on a "dial" and turned a handle. The device added or subtracted the numbers for him. But it could not multiply or divide.

In 1832, English mathematician and inventor Charles Babbage designed a calculating machine called the Analytical Engine. It was special because it worked by using a series of instructions in the form of a pattern of holes punched in a card—the "program." Unfortunately, a working machine was not built at the time.

The first electric computers

Babbage's idea for a programmable calculating machine was taken up by scientists in the 1930s and 1940s. But instead of using a mass of mechanical parts similar to those in Babbage's device, the scientists used electricity to make their machines work.

Charles Babbage (1792–1871) became professor of mathematics at Cambridge University, England, in 1828. His designs for mechanical computers included the Difference Engine and the more computer-like Analytical Engine.

The first programmable machine

In 1805, French engineer Joseph-Marie Jacquard invented a loom that could weave material with decorative designs from various colors of silk thread. What was remarkable about the machine was that instructions for each pattern were contained in cards with punched holes. These instruction cards were programs, and Jacquard's loom was the first automatic programmable machine.

Electric computers could store numbers and information in a memory. They had switches called relays, which clicked on and off when electricity passed through them. The Harvard Mark 1 of the late 1930s was a relay computer that could add, subtract, multiply, and divide very large numbers. It took about four seconds to do each calculation.

ENIAC

Electronic computers followed, which seemed to have no moving parts. Instead, they relied on tiny amounts of electricity passing along wires and through electronic devices. One of the first was Colossus, built in Great Britain in 1943. It was designed specially to crack secret German codes during World War II (1939–45). It was not fully programmable, so it was not a true, general-purpose computer.

The first device that we would recognize as a true computer was ENIAC (Electronic Numerical Integrator and Computer). It was built in 1945. ENIAC could store its own programs and data and could do about three hundred sums or calculations per second. However, it was very large—it filled two huge rooms and used as much electricity as ten family houses. Also, it was not programmed by pressing keys on a keyboard or by loading a magnetic disk or tape. Instead, people had to change the wires and connections between the computer's different parts. But ENIAC was a huge leap forward.

Part of the Analytical Engine was completed in 1910—thirty-nine years after Babbage's death. Babbage himself ran out of money and could not fund his research.

One of ENIAC's first tasks was a series of calculations in atomic physics. These would have taken one hundred scientists about a year to complete, using the normal mathematical methods of the time. ENIAC finished the calculations in two hours.

COMPUTERS COME OF AGE

ENIAC's developers display a few of the machine's 18,000 vacuum tubes. ENIAC was used to solve complex calculations from 1946 to 1955.

The transistor

At first, electronic computers had devices called vacuum tubes, which looked like light bulbs. These switched on and off and controlled the flow of pulses of electricity, but they got very hot and broke down often.

The next leap forward in computers was the invention of the transistor in 1948. This did a job similar to a vacuum tube, but it was much smaller (about the size of a baked bean), was more reliable, used far less electricity, and was cheaper to make. Now it was possible for computers to become smaller and more powerful. During the 1960s, companies and government organizations started to use them. Some computers were room-sized and were called mainframes. Smaller, desk-sized machines were known as minicomputers.

The silicon chip

The development of the integrated circuit, or silicon chip, in the 1970s meant that, once more, computer power leaped upward. At the same time the size and price of computers fell. The electronic printed circuits allowed hundreds of transistors to fit onto a tiny slice of silicon—the same mineral found in sand grains.

A fingertip dwarfs two integrated circuits, or silicon chips. Each chip contains the equivalent of thousands of transistors, resistors, and other electronic devices, all designed together, built-in, and integrated.

Computers were now so small and cheap that many more people could buy one. They were called microcomputers, since the main "chip," or microprocessor, was very small. One of the first successful integrated home computers for everyday use was the Apple II in 1977.

VLSI technology

During the 1980s, electronics engineers developed VLSI (Very Large Scale Integration) technology. Electronic integrated circuits equivalent to many thousands of transistors could fit onto a silicon chip smaller than a fingernail. Computers became more and more common for business, leisure, and the home. The idea of one's very own computer, the PC (personal computer), was born.

Most computers today use VLSI technology. They would seem like miracle machines to the first computer designers. Progress continues even faster, for today's new computer is almost out of date when it is taken out of its box.

In 1987, the Apple Macintosh II home computer set new standards for power and ease of use. Almost at once the IBM PS/2 (Personal System 2) was introduced. The race for better, faster computers continues today.

HOW COMPUTERS WORK

At the most basic level, computers use numbers, and there are only two of them. These are the binary numbers—0 and 1.

The basics of binary

Binary numbers look strange to us because we are used to the decimal counting system, which has ten digits: 1, 2, 3, 4, 5, 6, 7, 8, 9, and 0. When a decimal number has more than one digit, each digit to the left of the first one increases in value ten times. So in the decimal number 10, the 1 means ten. In binary, each digit to the left of the first one increases in value by two times. For example, in the binary number 10, the 1 means two. So binary 10 is the same as decimal 2.

All based on numbers

Computers represent information by pulses of electricity. The binary counting system is very useful, because in the computer, 0 is no electricity, or "off," while 1 is a pulse of electricity, or "on." All the different actions a computer performs are based on this on–off switching of electrical pulses.

In computers, the binary digits 1 and 0 are called bits, and these are grouped together into units called bytes. Nowadays, PCs have sixteen or thirty-two bits in one byte. The computer can add, subtract, and do many other kinds of arithmetic by changing the combinations of bits and bytes in its circuits. It can do this thousands of times each second.

Science students use computers to simulate, or mimic, the results of an experiment. They see diagrams, pictures, and words, but the basic language of the computer is binary.

Decimal number	Binary number
0	0
1	1
2	10
3	11
4	100
5	101
6	110
7	111
8	1000
9	1001
10	1010

Left We usually count and calculate using the decimal system, based on tens. Computers use the binary system, based on twos. It has only two digits, 0 and 1. One drawback is that more digits are needed for a number. Decimal number 9 has one digit; its binary equivalent is 1001, which has four digits.

Computer codes

Computers also deal with words, symbols, lines, and pictures. Inside the computer each of the various types of data is represented by a different code number that allows the computer to alter or store them. The exact code number that is used will depend on the type of computer code the machine uses.

For example, in the computer code called ASCII (American Standard Code for Information Interchange), the decimal number 1 is represented by the code number 49 or 110001 in binary. The letter A is represented by the code number 65 or 1000001 in binary. In ASCII, every number, letter, and dot in a picture is represented by one of its 128 codes.

Below ASCII codes represent various numbers, letters, and other keyboard symbols. They also code for simple instructions, such as ^G (control G), which sounds the beeper. The codes can be written in decimal, from 000 to 127, or in hexadecimal, a number system based on sixteens (0, 1, 2, 3, 4, 5, 6, 7, 8, 9, A, B, C, D, E, F).

ASCII code	Hex	Character	ASCII code	Hex	Character	ASCII code	Hex	Character
032	20	(space)	064	40	@	096	60	`
033	21	!	065	41	A	097	61	a
034	22	"	066	42	B	098	62	b
035	23	#	067	43	C	099	63	c
036	24	$	068	44	D	100	64	d
037	25	%	069	45	E	101	65	e
038	26	&	070	46	F	102	66	f
039	27	'	071	47	G	103	67	g
040	28	(	072	48	H	104	68	h
041	29	)	073	49	I	105	69	i
042	2A	*	074	4A	J	106	6A	j
043	2B	+	075	4B	K	107	6B	k
044	2C	,	076	4C	L	108	6C	l
045	2D	-	077	4D	M	109	6D	m
046	2E	.	078	4E	N	110	6E	n
047	2F	/	079	4F	O	111	6F	o
048	30	0	080	50	P	112	70	p
049	31	1	081	51	Q	113	71	q
050	32	2	082	52	R	114	72	r
051	33	3	083	53	S	115	73	s
052	34	4	084	54	T	116	74	t
053	35	5	085	55	U	117	75	u
054	36	6	086	56	V	118	76	v
055	37	7	087	57	W	119	77	w
056	38	8	088	58	X	120	78	x
057	39	9	089	59	Y	121	79	y
058	3A	:	090	5A	Z	122	7A	z
059	3B	;	091	5B	[	123	7B	{
060	3C	<	092	5C	\	124	7C	|
061	3D	=	093	5D	]	125	7D	}
062	3E	>	094	5E	^	126	7E	~
063	3F	?	095	5F	<	127	7F	(delete)

COMPUTER HARDWARE

Computers are made up of the parts that you can see, known as hardware, and the parts you cannot see—the tiny electrical pulses known as software or programs (see pages 14 and 15).

CPU The "heart" of a PC is the CPU (Central Processor Unit), a silicon chip about the size of your fingernail, contained within a protective box. Metal pins join it to connectors, linking it to other parts of the computer. The CPU splits everything the computer does into short, simple sums that it carries out at incredible speed.

RAM RAM (Random Access Memory) chips are the temporary "working memory" of a computer. RAM is blank when the computer is switched on, and it disappears when the computer is switched off. In use, the program the computer is using, plus any data put in by the user, is fed into it. The data in RAM chips can be read, that is, fed into the CPU, and then changed.

ROM The computer's "permanent memory" is stored on ROM (Read Only Memory). ROM contains the basic operating information, for example, that enables the computer to interpret signals coming in from the keyboard, and send signals to the screen. The CPU can read from ROM, but it cannot write to it or change it.

Nestling under the laptop's keyboard are dozens of microchips (integrated circuits) and other hardware components, packed together to save space, and constructed to save weight.

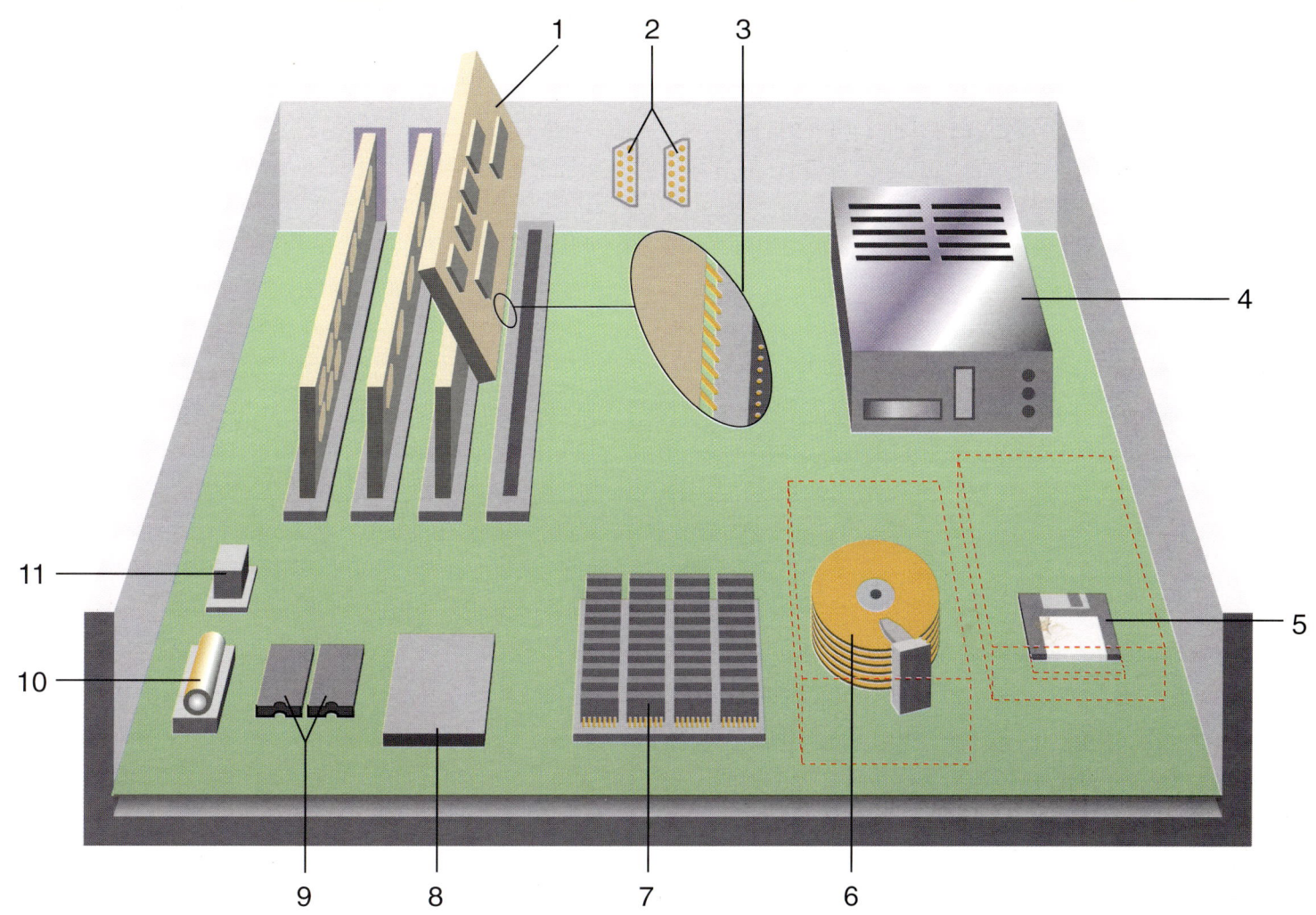

Clock All parts of the computer depend on knowing the exact passage of time, so that the millions of electronic signals can be passed around at the right speed and with the correct gaps between them. This is the job of the clock chip.

Transformer This is found in many electrical gadgets. It changes the powerful 120 volts of electricity from a wall outlet to 16 or fewer volts, as required by the various parts of the computer.

I/O cards The I/O (Input and Output) cards process signals coming in from various devices, such as the keyboard or mouse, and going out to other devices, such as a screen.

PCB Each set of chips and other components is mounted onto a PCB (Printed Circuit Board). It is a sheet of plastic-type material with connecting strips of metal that make electrical circuits.

Edge connectors The connections along the edge of the PCB slide into the edge connector, to link them to the rest of the computer.

Beneath the lid of a desktop computer are several sets of circuit boards with chips and other components. This is the computer hardware. There are usually empty slots and spaces to add extra chips and boards (cards), such as more RAM chips.

1. ROM and other chips on PCBs
2. Ports (for plugging in other devices)
3. Edge connectors along edge of PCB
4. Transformer and power supply circuits
5. Floppy disk drive
6. Hard disk drive
7. RAM chips
8. CPU chip
9. BIOS (Basic Input/Output System) chips
10. Back-up battery for clock
11. Clock chip

13

COMPUTER SOFTWARE

Software cannot be seen because it is made up of tiny pulses of electricity moving around inside the computer. The main kind of software is the program that a computer uses to do various jobs. There are thousands of programs, covering almost every task you can imagine—games, writing, compiling a database, making calculations, and drawing. These types of programs are usually called applications.

Applications

The applications used with a computer usually come stored on a magnetic tape or disk, or a CD-ROM (see page 16). They are a sequence of instructions, which is loaded into the computer's memory.

An integrated circuit contains a microscopic maze of electronic devices. Pulses of electricity pass through the maze, representing binary digits or bits of the binary number system.

Operating system

Another type of program is called the operating system. An example is DOS (Disk Operating System). This controls the computer's most basic functions, such as ensuring the CPU works correctly, responding to the signals from the keyboard, and sending out the right signals to the monitor screen. In many computers, the operating system is stored in ROM chips. It loads itself automatically (sometimes called "booting up") when the computer is turned on.

Programming languages

Applications, operating systems, and all other kinds of programs are written by computer programmers, using computer programming languages. There are dozens of these languages, each suited to a certain kind of computing. The most basic is the zeros and ones of binary. This is called machine code. The next steps up are assembly and compiler languages, which are slightly faster and easier for programmers to use. The high-level or symbolic languages, such as BASIC and LOGO, are the ones people understand best. As the programmer writes in a high-level language, it is translated by the computer into a low-level language, such as machine code.

Even smaller than a laptop, the modern palmtop has more computing power than a desktop machine of ten years ago. It links to other computers to "download" its information.

Popular programming languages

- FORTRAN (FORmula TRANslator) was the first widely used high-level language, for the complicated arithmetic of engineering and science. It was created in 1956.
- BASIC (Beginner's All-purpose Symbolic Instruction Code) was designed in 1965 especially for beginners and home users to write their own programs.
- "C" is quick to write and makes good use of the computer's time and memory. It was first available in the 1970s.
- LOGO helps young children learn about numbers, computers, and simple programming. It was designed in the 1970s.
- PROLOG (PROgramming LOGic) is a powerful language used to program the next generation of super computers. It first came into use in the 1980s.

COMPUTER INPUT DEVICES

Magnified 2,000 times, the tiny pits on a compact disc show as red-yellow stripes in the green plastic layer. The clear, protective plastic layer on top is shown in blue.

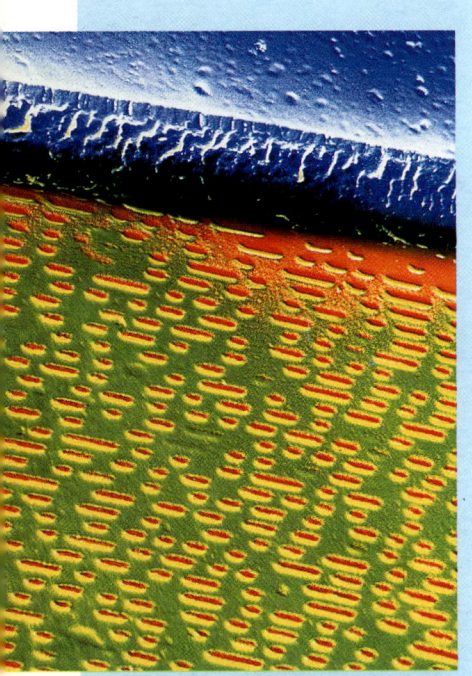

CD-ROMs
These discs have microscopic pits and bumps on their metal-coated surfaces. When a laser beam shines on them and is reflected in a certain way, an electronic pulse is triggered. Though information can be copied from a CD-ROM to a computer, information from a computer cannot be copied to the CD-ROM.

A typical PC can do nothing without human instruction. Even downloading its operating system cannot be done by the computer alone. A person must tell it to do so. A person must turn on the power switch.

The power switch is just one of the many input devices used to communicate instructions to a computer. These devices transform certain kinds of information into electronic impulses that prompt a computer to perform various functions. Each form of information has an input device especially for it.

Keyboard This has a set of keys that you press to type a word or a number. Each press of a key, or keystroke, sends a short burst of signals along the cable that attaches it to the computer. Each key has its own code of signals.

Mouse A handheld device that sends signals to the computer when it is moved. The signals are translated into the movements of an arrow on the screen. One or more clicks of the button send coded signals to the computer.

Magnetic disk drive This is a device for input, storage, and output. Information is stored as patterns of tiny magnetic patches. These patches are detected by the magnetic head, which slides across the disk, and turned into digital electronic signals (see panel).

CD-ROM drive This is a memory device that uses a CD-ROM (Compact Disc-Read Only Memory), to read information (see panel).

Joystick Moving the joystick handle presses a switch hidden in its base, sending streams of electronic pulses along the cable into the computer.

Scanner A device used to copy images into the computer (see page 33).

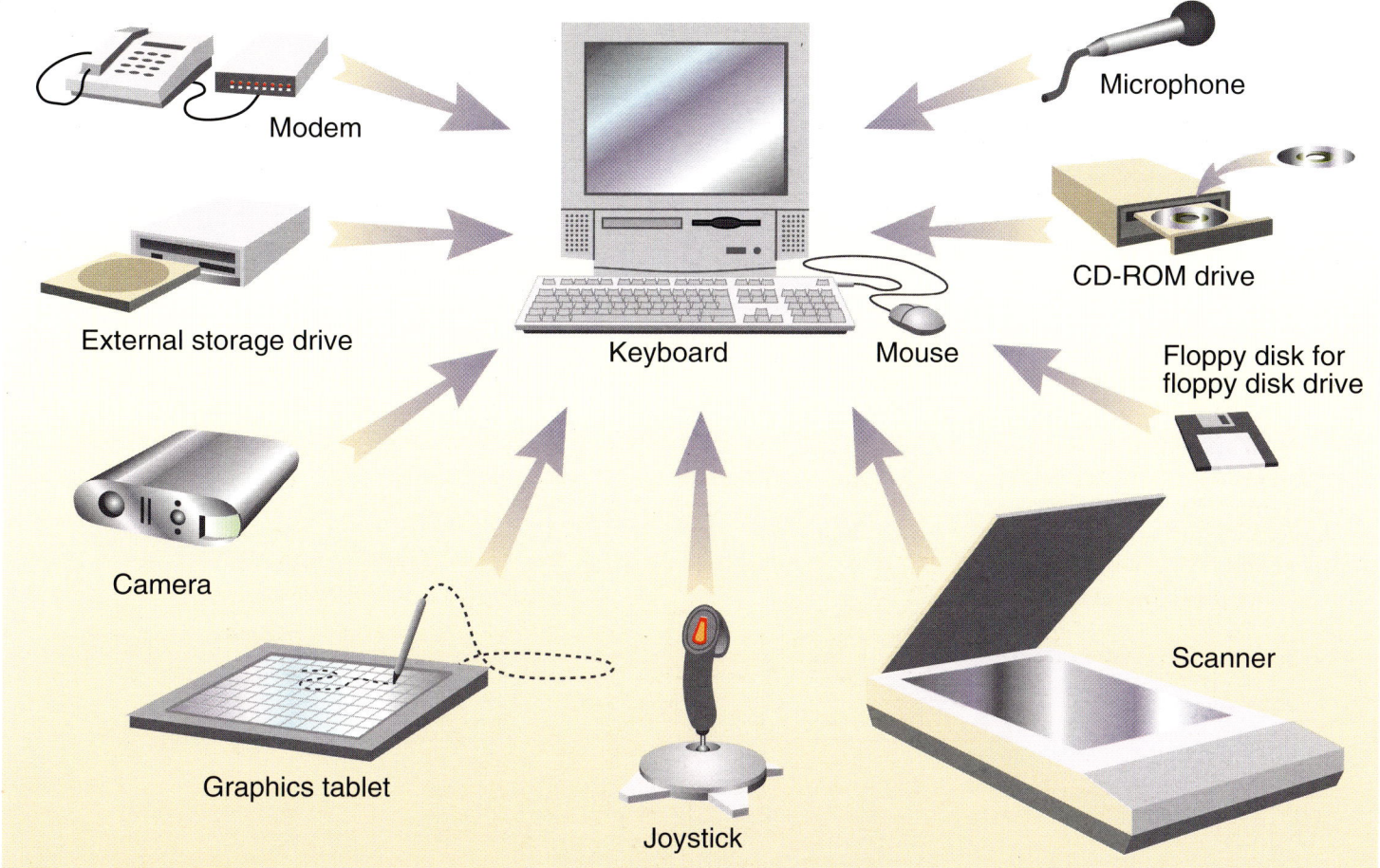

Graphics tablet A device used mainly to draw pictures on the computer screen (see pages 23 and 31).

Microphone The microphone converts sound waves into "waves" of electricity. These are analog electrical signals (see panel). They are changed into digital electronic signals for the computer.

Camera Instead of recording an image on film, a computer's camera converts images into digital electrical signals the computer can read (see page 33).

Most desktop computers can accept input from a variety of devices, but not at the same time. Different programs are needed to accept and interpret the signals from the devices so the computer can understand them. The keyboard and mouse programs are usually a standard part of the computer's system.

Analog and digital

Modern computers are digital. They use the digits of the binary code (see page 10). Many older computers and other devices use the analog system. To understand the difference between these systems, assume a person wants to send a signal to a computer meaning "7."

In the analog system, "7" could be represented by one pulse of seven volts. However, it is very difficult to get a pulse of exactly seven volts—it might be a little more (or less) than seven volts. The digital system overcomes this problem. In the digital system, "7" would be three pulses of one volt each—111 (the binary version of the decimal number 7). This system does not vary continuously like the analog system. It is simply on or off, so it leaves less room for error.

COMPUTER OUTPUT DEVICES

This man and woman are using keyboards and special, transparent mice to transfer blueprints into the computer. The computer's interpretation of the input can be seen on their computer screens, one of the many output devices used by computers.

Output devices take the electronic pulses put out by the computer and change them into a readable form. The most common output device is the monitor, or screen. Some output devices are not used directly by people. The output signals may, for example, instruct a robot to paint or to tighten screws.

The monitor

The computer monitor alone operates similarly to a television set. But the electronic circuits in a computer monitor respond to signals from the computer, which are very different from the signals sent by a television transmitter. But a computer video circuit or card can make the television's signals acceptable for a computer monitor, so the computer monitor can be used as a television.

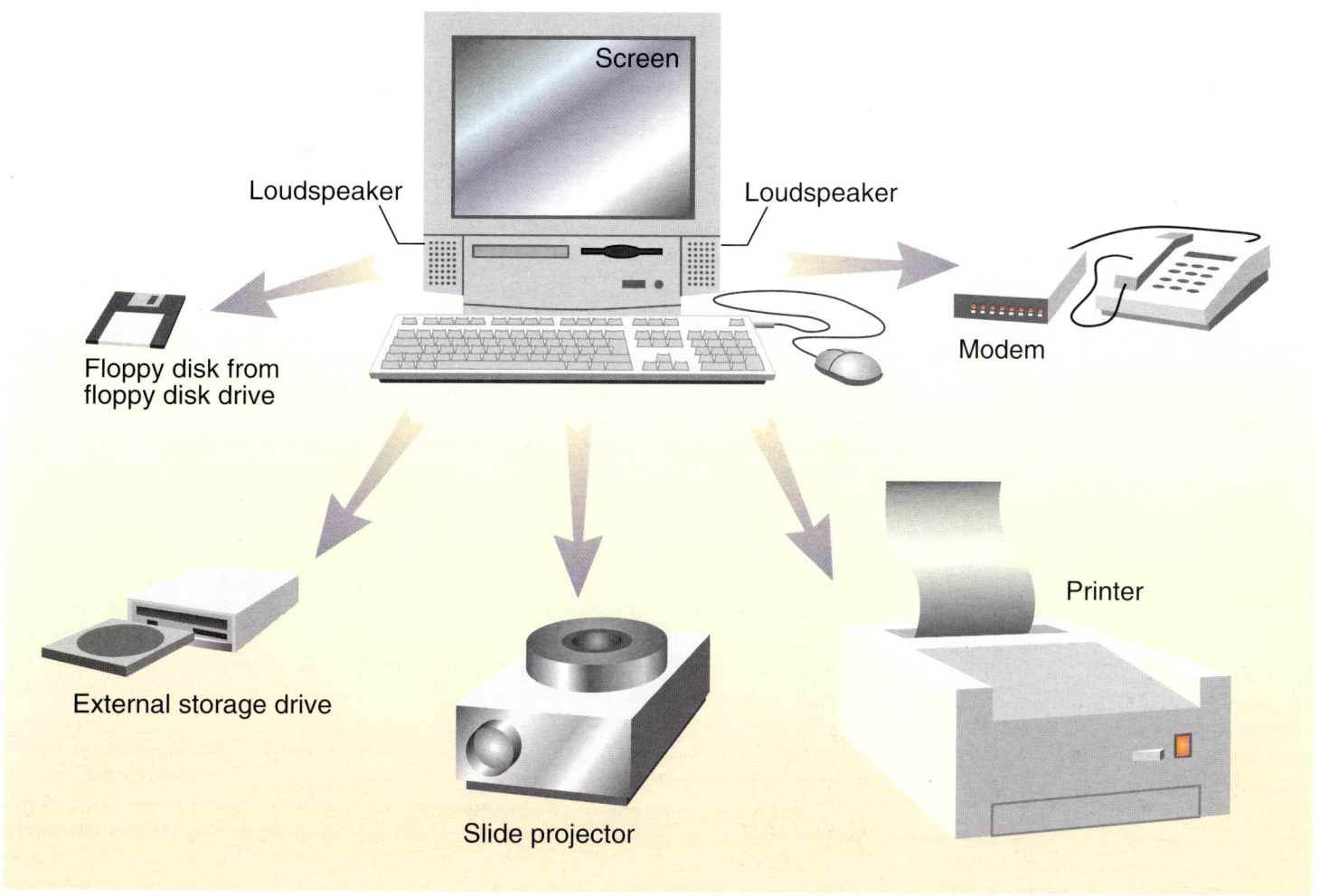

Monitor The monitor, or VDU (Visual Display Unit), changes the computer's output into patterns of light to form words, numbers, symbols, pictures, and so on.

Speaker This turns electrical signals into sound. It makes the "beeps" and "dings" that show the computer is working correctly, and it plays music and sound effects from the computer.

Printer The printer turns the electronic signals from the computer into patterns of ink on paper or card. There are many kinds of printers available. Most print only one color (usually black); others can print many colors.

Magnetic disk drive This is a device for input, storage, and output (see page 16).

The typical PC has a monitor and disk drive, plus a speaker. In order for certain other output devices, such as printers or slide projectors, to be operated from a computer, special programs need to be loaded into the computer.

The modem

A modem (modulator-demodulator) changes the electronic signals inside the computer into coded signals suitable for passing along the telephone lines of the telecommunications network. At the other end, the signals are converted by the modem of the receiving computer. In this way, modems allow computers to "talk" on the telephone. Modems operate at different speeds. The speed is determined by how fast the modem is able to transfer information.

GAMES AND ENTERTAINMENT

Arcade machines offer games of all kinds, from fantasy and science-fiction adventure to discovery and simulation. Many home PCs also produce similar-quality, high-speed graphics.

During the 1980s, computer games were the fastest growing of all toys and games. By the 1990s, people began to expect still bigger, better, more complicated games. However, these were more expensive and fewer were sold.

Some computer games are pre-programmed in machines designed specifically for them. The game program is contained in a ROM chip. The machine can do little else except run the game. However, it is hardly a computer, because it is not easily programmed to do other tasks. Usually, the only option is to "plug in" another game, by exchanging the cartridge containing the ROM chip.

Some computer games are designed for use on multipurpose computers. These games can be complicated, with many options for setting up and playing. You can choose a mouse, joystick, or keyboard as your input device and can play against another person or the computer itself. There are often various levels of difficulty, and some games can take several months to complete or win.

The computer game industry has adapted many existing games, sports, and pastimes. Familiar card and board games, such as solitaire and chess, can be played on computers. In 1988, the computer company IBM developed Deep Thought, the first computer program to play against a chess expert and win. In 1996, the Deep Blue computer program won some games against the world chess champion, though it lost the match overall.

Soccer, basketball, golf, and many other sports can now be played on computers. A person can even simulate fishing or hang gliding on a computer. Each year the games become more complex and lifelike.

Types of computer games

- **Role-playing.** This allows players to become other people, real or imaginary, and see how they face challenges and solve problems.
- **Shoot-'em-ups.** These are games involving weapons, destruction, damage, and death. They range from ancient contests with spears and swords, through western gunfights and modern machine gun battles, to futuristic space attacks with lasers and photon torpedoes.
- **Simulations.** These games simulate or mimic lifelike situations. They allow a player to see how he/she copes with running a huge industrial corporation or flying a jetliner.
- **Fantasy.** These are games involving mystery and magic, sorcery and spells, castles and jewels, ancient stone tablets and medieval scrolls, and dungeons and dragons.

Even game flight simulators use massive amounts of computer-processing power for real-time display. The main input here is the flight deck control column—better known as the joystick.

MOVIEMAKING

In 1982, Disney's *Tron* became the first full-length movie based on computer graphics. It used images generated by computer programs combined with film of real actors and objects. It was set inside the electronic circuits of a computer, as the hero battled to escape to the outside world.

Disney's movie *Tron* introduced futuristic designs and images to create a "computerscape" world, with dramatic scenes set inside the electronic circuits of the machine.

Computers have gradually become more important in moviemaking. They can copy a scene and add, or fill in parts, that are not exactly right. Used in combination with models, artwork, and other techniques, they can produce startling special effects, such as the dinosaurs in *Jurassic Park*.

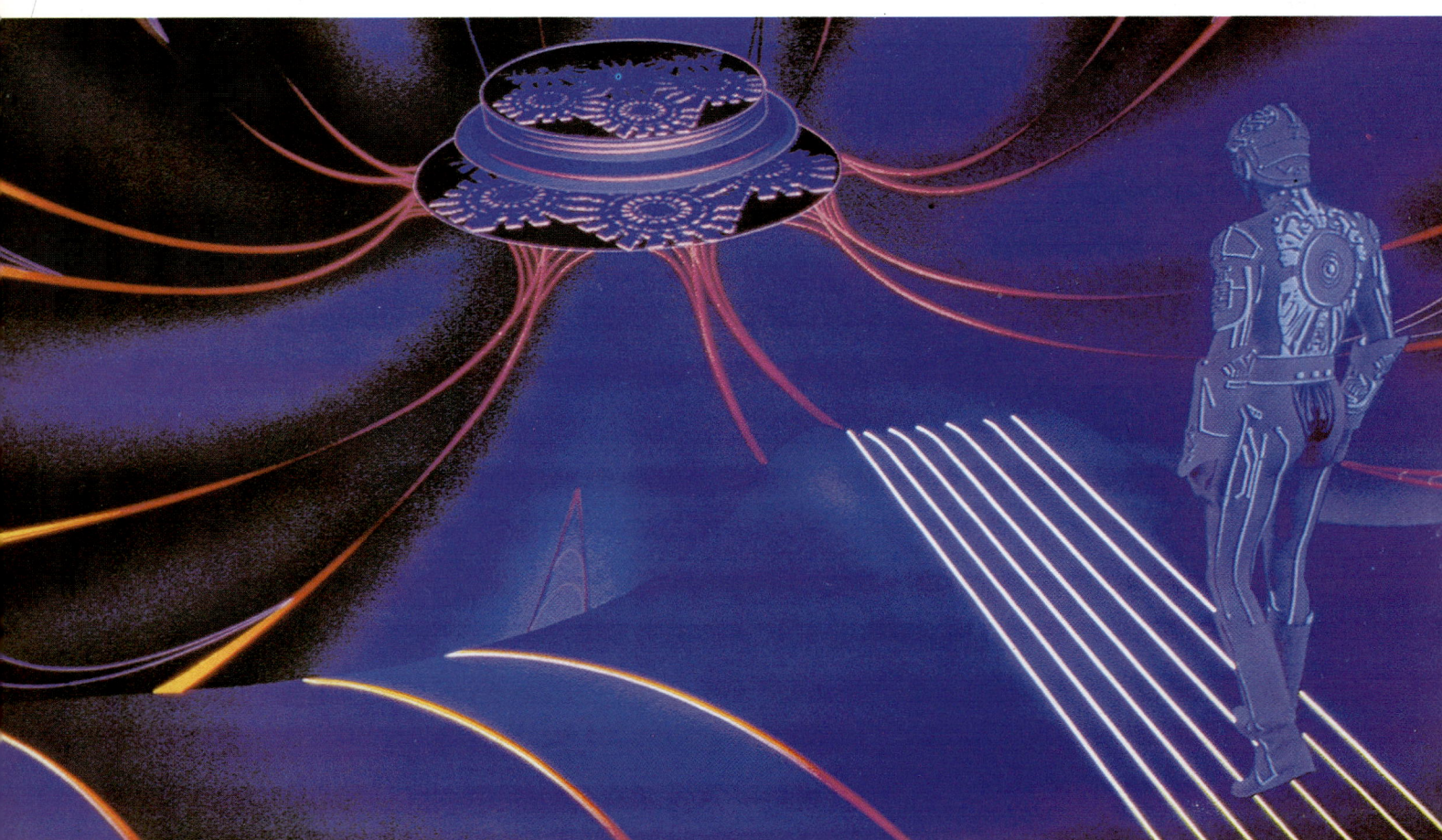

In 1995, Disney produced *Toy Story*, the world's first full-length animated film made entirely by computer. It lasts for seventy-seven minutes and has 110,000 individual frames, or still images, of film. To produce that number of frames, a large team of people working with dozens of computers used the equivalent of more than ninety years of computer time.

One of the computer's main jobs is to detect "gaps" between different elements in a scene, such as a cartoon animal moving in front of a real person. The computer scans the whole sequence into its memory. Then, using a graphics tablet on one of the still images, the operator removes the unwanted gaps by filling them with the right color. The correct lines and shadows are also added by hand to make realistic edges. The computer is programmed to do a similar job on the rest of the scene by itself for each of the frames that follow, at more than twenty each second. It does this so well that when the film is shown, the scene is flawless.

A scene from the full-length film *Toy Story*. The animation was done entirely by computer.

COMPUTERS AND VIRTUAL REALITY

To experience VR (virtual reality), a user usually sits in a mounted chair near a screen or wears a headset, puts on special gloves, or holds handsets. Sensors attached to these input devices detect the movements of the user's head, neck, hands, and other body parts and relay the information back to the computer. The headset, which is the computer's output device, shows the user a scene generated by the computer. Sounds heard by the user are produced by the computer.

Into the computer world of virtual reality: by putting on the headset with 3D vision and stereo sound, the user is transported to the cockpit of a race car. Only the smells of fuel and burning rubber are missing.

The movements of the headset and racket are tracked by sensors so that the player sees himself moving around the court and swinging his racket, almost as in real life.

VR transports the user into another world. "Virtual" means it has the appearance and effect of being real but, in fact, is not. It exists only as codes of electronic pulses in the computer, or "cyberspace." It relays information as images, sounds, and motions (and in some systems, smells and touch, too). The user experiences these through his or her senses and recreates the virtual world in his brain.

During the 1990s, improved computer power made VR games more widely available. For a coin in the slot, the user can stalk aliens through the landscape of another world or fly a jet fighter on a dangerous mission.

In a massively complex music performance, computers help control sounds mixed from dozens of separate channels and work the lasers and other lights.

Light and sound

Computers are used in modern shows such as music concerts and in theater. They control the lights as they switch lighting effects, such as lasers, spot beams, and stroboscopes, on and off at precisely the right moments.

Computers are also used to alter and even create sounds and music. The synthesizer makes its own sounds, which the operator changes by using various electronic controls. Some sounds are based on samples or recordings of real instruments. Others are computer generated and are familiar from the sound tracks of space and fantasy movies. They are stored on disk or in ROM and are usually activated by playing the keyboard.

EDUCATION AND TRAINING

In this museum, visitors view fossils, skeletons, and animal exhibits with the help of a computer terminal linked to the Internet.

When PCs first became widely available, many people thought they would be used mainly for business or pleasure. However, a new use has gradually developed—education.

In countries such as Great Britain and the United States, almost every school has at least one computer of some kind. Large colleges and universities have many of them. Computers are now an established part of the learning process, used by everyone from the very young just learning to count to university students taking their final examinations. They also help people to learn about computers themselves, and how to operate them. Computer literacy—knowing what they do and how to use them—has become an important skill.

Young and old

One advantage of the computer as a learning tool is that it is very adaptable. The same computer can help five-year-olds with simple spelling, and then, using a different program, it can test student doctors or engineers.

Another advantage is space. Compared with more traditional teaching materials, such as books, a computer's magnetic disks or CD-ROMs hold incredible amounts of information. Almost a whole shelf of encyclopedias, including words and pictures, fits onto one CD-ROM.

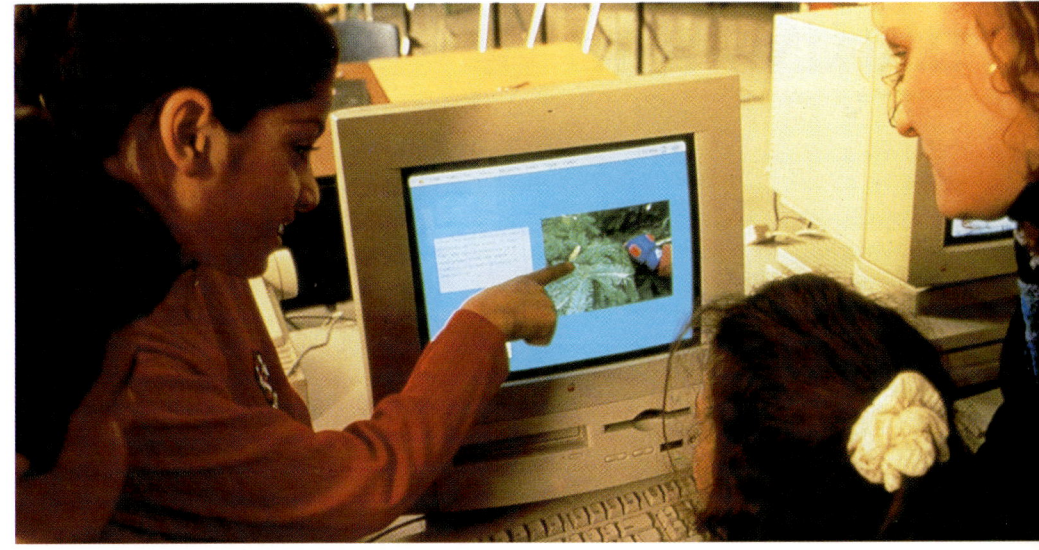

Interactive multimedia computers respond to our actions, using graphics, animation, and sounds. They make learning fun and more effective, too.

Learning can be fun

Modern multimedia computers produce a whole variety of words, moving pictures, sounds, and music. They enable people to learn by looking, listening, and doing.

The same elements of discovery and fun used in computer games can be used in education. Users are more likely to remember a famous speech if the historical person "comes alive" on screen to make it, or to learn about an important invention if they follow the steps the inventor made in arriving at the new device.

However, computers are unlikely to replace all traditional methods of teaching. They are good for some types of learning, but not for others. Some users get carried away with the "game" and learn very little. Nevertheless, the computer has taken its place alongside books and chalkboards as an important tool of education.

TRAINING WITH VR

Games that use VR have become widespread only recently. However, some types of VR have been used for many years. Airplane pilots train on a simulator, which is a type of VR machine. They see views of the airport, sky, and landscape as they take off and land. If they crash, it is certainly less dangerous and less costly than destroying a real plane.

The flight simulator computer projects the view seen by the pilot onto the large curved mirror (right). It also works hydraulic rams (above) that make the simulator cabin tilt, lean, and vibrate, to mimic the movements of a real airplane.

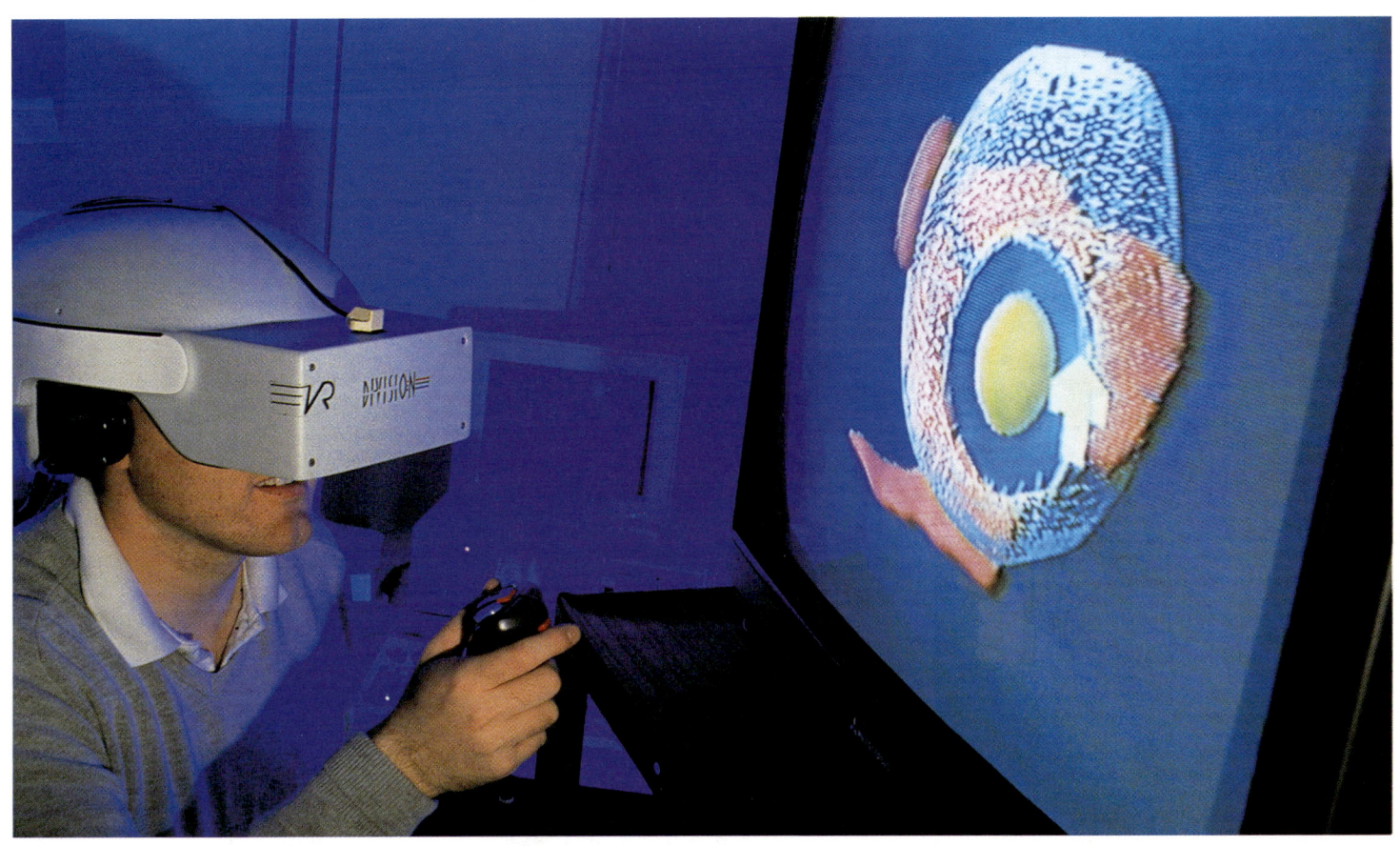

A flight simulator is extremely expensive and uses huge amounts of computing power. A full 360-degree color image of a giant landscape must be stored in the computer, which takes up a lot of memory. The pilot only ever sees a small part of it, but it changes many times a second as the computer responds to the user's actions and gaze. This is coupled with changing sounds in the headphones, movements of the chair, and flight control devices. Taken together, these effects make the experience seem realistic.

There are VR training systems available for many different professions. A surgeon, for example, can practice operations without endangering life by operating on a virtual human body. As the surgeon works, motion sensors track the scalpel and other instruments. The computer monitors them, cuts away skin, muscles, and other tissues as instructed (all from information stored in its memory) and relays out the results as images to the headset. VR is also used to train firefighters, deep-sea divers, and other professionals and is used by sports people such as skiers and hang glider pilots.

An eye surgeon practices an operation using a virtual reality headset and joystick. Inside the headset, he sees a three-dimensional view of the scene, shown on the monitor for the benefit of spectators.

ART AND DESIGN

Since the 1960s, people have explored the creative side of computing. This means getting the computer itself to create or make up something—a pattern, picture, story, or even a piece of music. Of course, someone must write a program to enable the computer to carry out such tasks.

In general, the results have not amazed the world. Most computer art seems very "mechanical"—it is too regular and perfectly done to inspire the imagination.

This picture of a "human" shooting through rainbow hoops was made using a computer. Many consider computer art to be uninspiring.

Drawing with computers

It is possible to draw by computer using a mouse, but this is often awkward and feels unnatural. With an input device known as a graphics tablet, a person uses a special pen or stylus, and what is drawn appears on the computer's monitor. One type detects the pressure of the pen touching the tablet pad. Another type senses the nearby presence of the metal stylus, which does not actually have to touch the tablet at all.

The tablet is constructed like a sheet of graph paper with tiny rows and columns making squares. The tablet detects the position of the pen, such as the fifty-third row along and fourteenth column up, and sends this as a code to the computer, which translates it into an equivalent position on the monitor.

A designer considers the computerized sketch of an automobile on the monitor. Computers aid design in many areas, from vehicles and aircraft to buildings, bridges, and dams.

COMPUTER DESIGN

In the architect's office, the plans of houses, buildings, and roads are traced by the mouse and fed into the computer. Once the basic information is stored, the designer can alter dimensions, curves, and other features, and see the results in a few seconds.

Many architects and designers now use a computer system instead of a traditional drawing board. The computer draws lines and curves with amazing accuracy. It can cut out the boredom of drawing many similar items, such as seats in an aircraft or rooms in a skyscraper, by carrying out a process called "step-and-repeat," which duplicates the items as often as required.

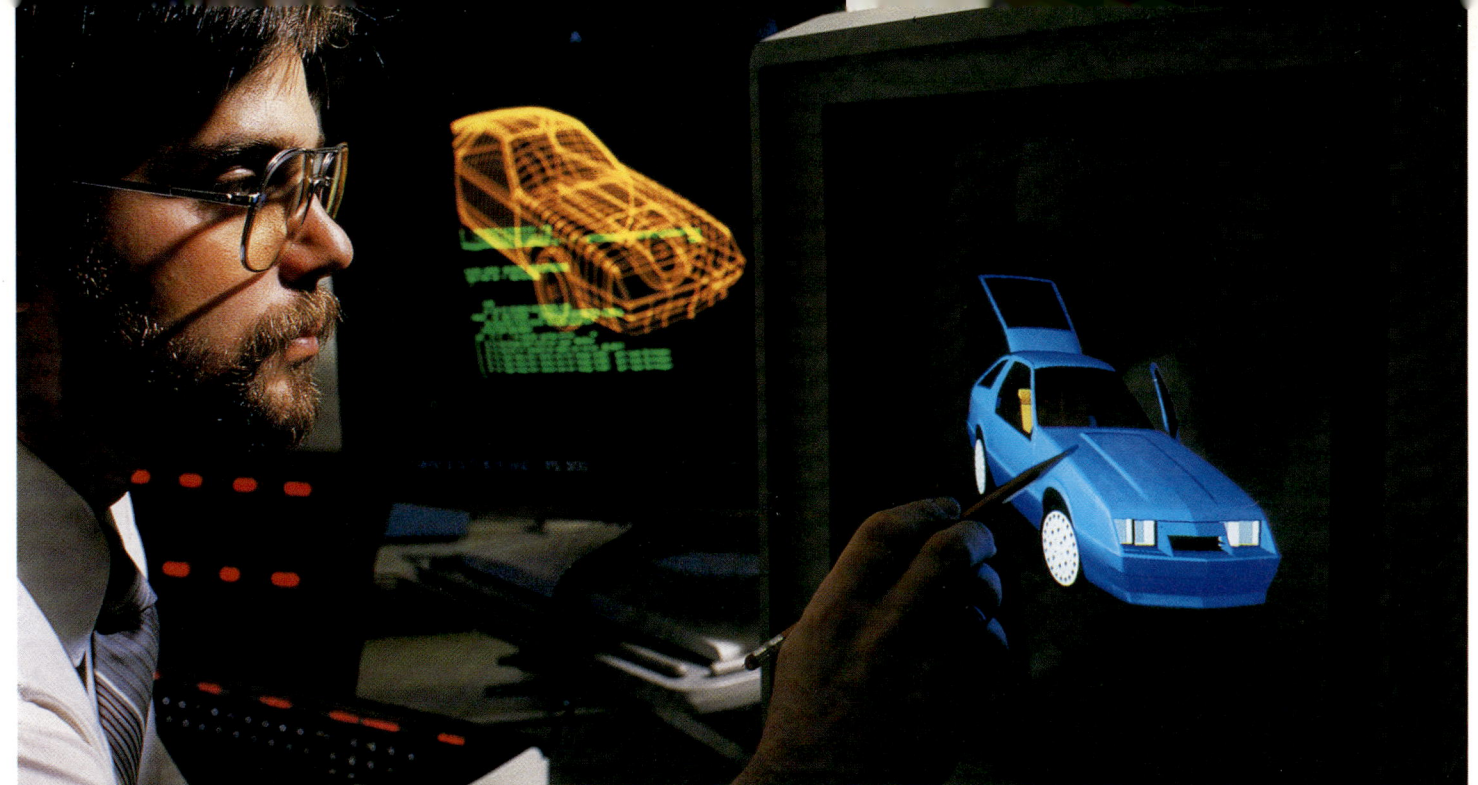

An engineer points out a detail on the plans for a new car. The vehicle can be twisted, turned, and viewed from any angle and cut away to show the insides—yet so far, no actual part of the car has been built.

CAD (Computer-Aided Design) systems can also give the impression of three dimensions, with depth added to the usual height and width. The measurements, or coordinates, of an object such as a chair—its edges, curves, corners, lines, and surfaces—are fed into the computer memory. The computer can then turn or rotate the object, to show it from above, the side, or the back. In a few minutes, the designer can produce a complex shape, such as a vehicle, a piece of furniture, or a building, and view it from any angle. Before CAD, this would have taken many days of pen-and-paper drawings and model making.

Scanners

A scanner turns a picture or image into patterns of electronic signals that can be changed or altered by the computer. The scanning "head" of this device moves across the image in a straight line, detecting patches of light and dark as it goes, and converts them into the electronic pulses. The head then moves to scan another line just below the first, and so on, hundreds of times. Any kind of image can be scanned—black-and-white prints, color slides, paintings, and drawings. But some scanners only produce a black-and-white digitized image, while others can produce both black-and-white and color pictures.

Cameras for computers

A computer camera contains an electronic part called a CCD (Charge Coupled Device). When light shines on this, it produces tiny signals of electricity in the same pattern as the pattern of light. The signals feed into the computer as codes of digital pulses ready for processing and use. This is called "digitizing the image."

THE WORKPLACE

Without computers, a modern business would screech to a halt in seconds. Computers do dozens of different jobs, such as processing orders for items, credit card accounts, bills and payments, and controlling stock.

Consider a visit to the local supermarket to buy the latest computer magazine, and imagine how many computers are involved. At the register, the cashier runs the magazine past a bar code reader. The bar code is a set of thick and thin black stripes that contains coded information—the name of the product, its identification number, price, date or origin, plus much more. This information passes into the supermarket's computer system, along with the information from hundreds of other items sold at all the other registers every minute.

The register computer terminal controls the laser beam bar code reader, displays item code numbers and prices, adds the subtotals and totals, and even prints the receipt.

Computers control the amount of inventory held in the supermarket warehouse, and pay for the cost of the items by EFT.

Stocks and orders

The details of each item sold are sent, or downloaded, from the supermarket's own computer to the central computer for the whole supermarket chain. This computer determines how many items, in each of the thousands of product lines, have been sold. It sends orders for new items to the many different suppliers and wholesalers.

These fresh supplies are delivered to the supermarket's central warehouse. The computer prints instructions showing how many of each should be delivered to the separate store sites, to keep the shelves stocked. This is known as inventory control. Computers also pay the bills for these fresh items, by a type of electronic banking called EFT (Electronic Fund Transfer).

Staff records and payments

At the end of the supermarket's day, the cashiers visit the staff room. From the staff schedules held on computer, they can see how many days' vacation are due to them and their work schedules for the coming weeks. Some employees also check that they have been paid by the computer payroll system, which deposits their salaries directly into their bank accounts.

COMPUTER-CONTROLLED MACHINES

Air traffic controllers use their monitors and radar screens to schedule aircraft landings and takeoffs. Many computers are at work behind the scenes, organizing flights and double-checking information.

Computers are in charge of millions of machines, from jumbo jets to dishwashers. Of course, they are not in total command. They follow the programs and instructions given to them by their human masters. Computers themselves vary enormously in complexity.

The computer system in a modern airplane or ship may have the processing power of five hundred home computers. The small control chip in a dishwasher is little more than a set of miniaturized switches that turn the water valve, pump, heater, and other devices on and off in the correct sequence. Televisions, washing machines, ovens, microwaves, stereos, cars, and many other machines use similar chips.

Much larger computer control systems are involved in launching a satellite into orbit or helping to run air traffic control at a busy airport.

Double checking

Certain types of computers are programmed to do many routine small tasks automatically. In air traffic control, they check that the airport radar systems are working properly and remind the controllers of regular flights. But they also identify problems and warn of difficulties, by double checking. If two planes are allowed to prepare for landing too close to each other, the computer flashes a warning.

However, any computer is only as good as the humans who built and programmed it. So human failing can lead to computer failure and, occasionally, disaster.

In touch-screen technology, the monitor screen responds to touches in certain areas. Press a panel on the screen, and it may enlarge for a more detailed view, or bring up a further list of options.

On an automobile assembly line, the robot windshield-fitter does not respond to spoken commands, but to electronic ones from its controlling computer.

Computers and robots

One type of robot is a machine with a computer "brain" that can carry out tasks that would otherwise have to be done by people. On an automotive production line, a robotized paint-sprayer puts exactly the right amounts of paint in the correct places. First it is "taught" by a human, who programs the movements into the computer's memory. Or the person moves the robot sprayer arm in the right way, and the computer detects the movements by feedback motion sensors in the arm.

After this, the robot sprayer works day and night. It never gets bored or distracted. Its work never varies unless the program is changed. Computer-controlled robot machines do hundreds of similar tasks for factories and industry, including the assembly of electronic circuits for more computers.

COMPUTER MAPS

Using data from land surveys and satellite photographs, a computer tilts the normal two-dimensional plan or map. This reveals the hills, valleys, and contours of the landscape, shaded to give the effect of three dimensions.

Computers are vital tools in mapmaking. Billions of pieces of information are beamed down from hundreds of satellites orbiting the earth. They represent images of the earth's surface, photographed and digitized, then transmitted as radio signals. Information in this form is ideal for a computer. It can plot a map of the landscape in its memory and tilt it to show hills, valleys, and other features from different viewpoints. Many people use these computer maps, from geologists looking for coal and oil to generals planning a battle.

What happens if . . . ?

One common question for computer modeling is "What happens if …?" Changes can be made to a computer model to find their possible effects. A computer model of city center traffic flow might predict the effects of altering traffic lights to a rotary or making a new one-way system. This saves the huge costs and disruption of doing it for real.

Medical scans

A standard X ray shows the bones inside the body as a flat, two-dimensional picture. But medical scanners show amazing details of softer parts, such as nerves and muscles. They are able to show the body in thin "slices," or as a three-dimensional image that can be rotated. The medical scanner itself takes thousands of pictures through the body at different levels and angles. The computer combines and builds them into the final image.

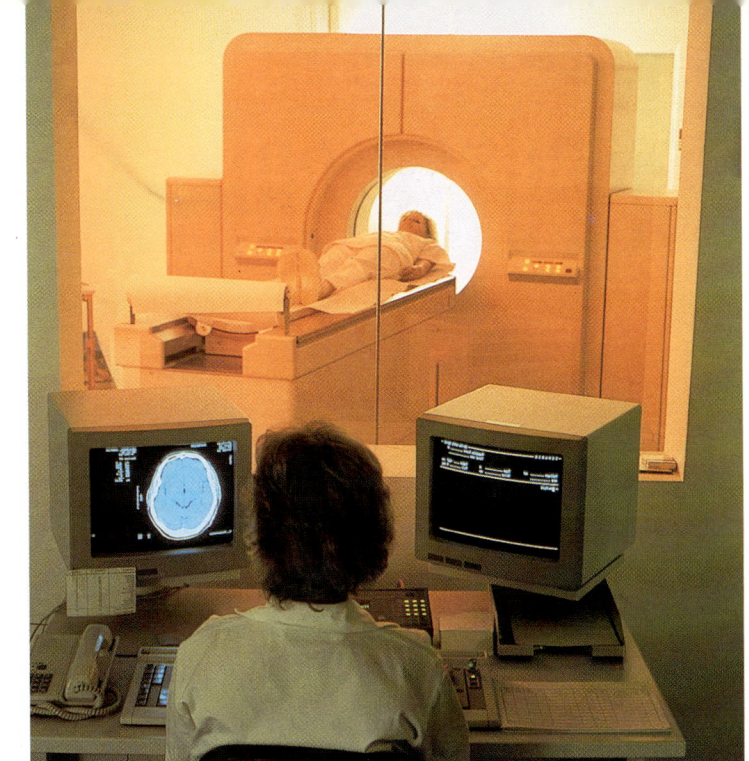

A patient undergoes a brain scan in the hospital. The scanner and computer work together to build slice-by-slice images through the body into a three-dimensional version.

Computer modeling

Tomorrow's weather forecast was produced not by looking at seaweed, but by a huge computer with the processing power of thousands of PCs.

In addition to the weather, big computers are used to figure out many complicated events and processes. Some try to predict the future, such as the ups and downs of business markets; the effects of disease and famine on human populations; the workings of nature, such as the numbers of fish in a lake or deer in a forest; and the results of an imaginary nuclear explosion or an earthquake. From the predictions, people are helped in various ways, such as enabling business managers to plan the growth of their companies, and rescue services to organize their response to natural disasters.

Other computers look at events that have already occurred. They are recreated in the computer and studied in detail to see how they happened. This is called computer modeling or simulation.

Satellite photographs and information from weather stations are processed by the computer and displayed on monitors. The meteorologist (weather expert) interprets the results into the more familiar weather map.

COMPUTER CRIME

Computer crime is very common. Copying computer games and other programs without the permission of the makers is against the law. This is called pirating.

Software pirates make thousands of illegal copies and sell them. They sometimes even copy the packaging. This costs the computer industry an estimated $15 billion each year. Hardware pirates make copies of famous makes of computers and equipment, again without permission.

Stolen goods

In the United States alone, computer crime involves an estimated $100 billion each year. One form is simply stealing computers, disks, and equipment. For their size and weight, they are valuable pieces of machinery. Some criminals open the computer to remove the chips that are inside, which are literally worth more than their weight in gold.

Before this user could get into the company computer system, he had to type in a secret password and entry codes.

Computer hacking

Hackers are people who get into computer systems where they should not be. Most hackers work from small computers connected by a modem into the telecommunications network. They dial into a company or organization and figure out the passwords and secret codes that are supposed to give protection. Once through this security gateway, they have access to personal and business information that could be very valuable.

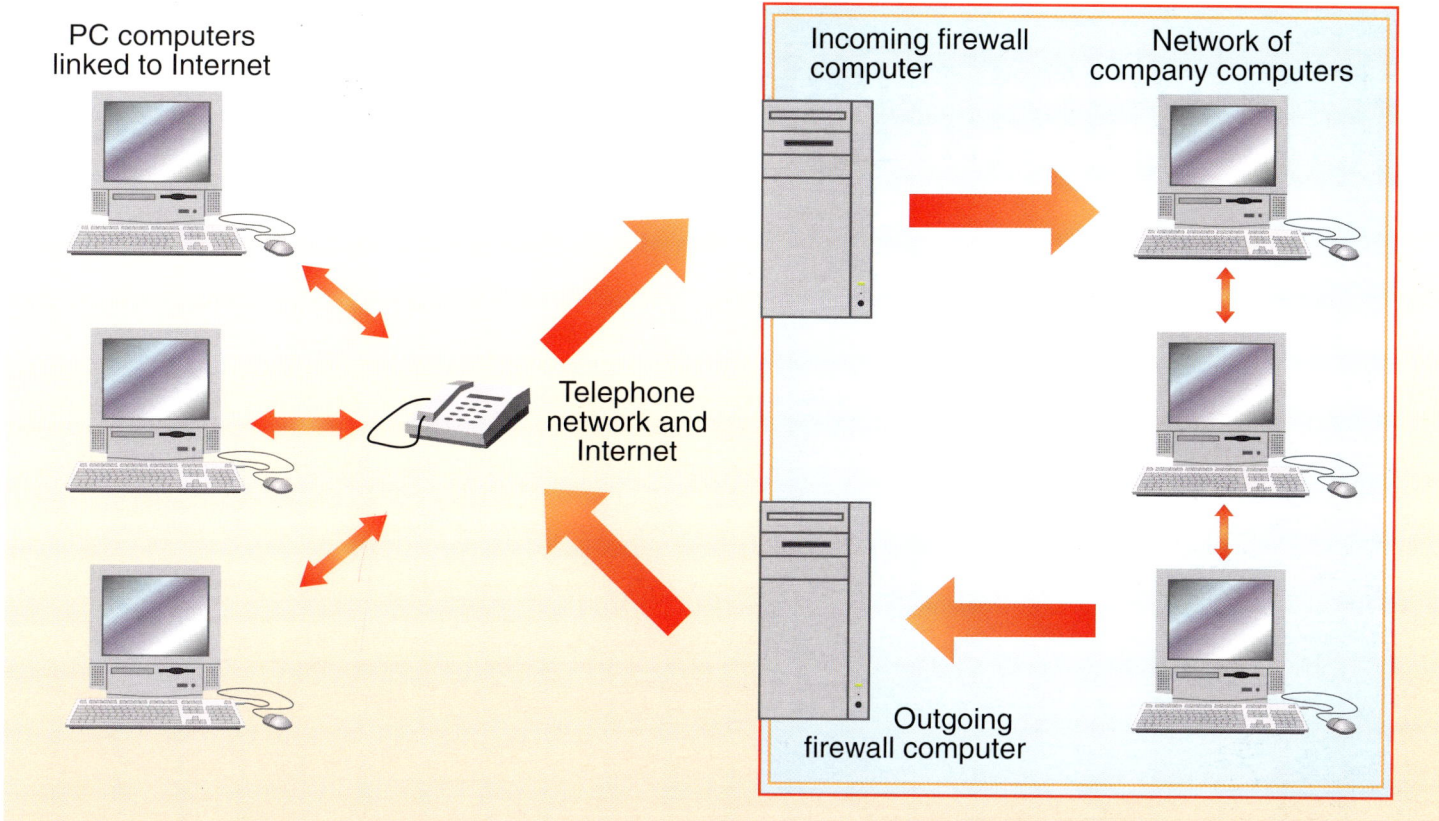

Some hackers simply want to beat computer security systems. It is a challenge. Others take money by sending it electronically to secret bank accounts. Or they extract information and sell it to rivals, or use it for fraud, blackmail, and other crimes.

The rising tide of computer crime

Opening a letter addressed to someone else without that person's consent is against the law. The same applies to information sent along telephone lines between computers, for example, in the form of electronic mail, or E-mail.

Another computer crime is distributing material that might be highly indecent, racially abusive, or otherwise against the law. However, so much information flashes around the world among millions of computer users on the Internet and other systems, that it is difficult to catch the criminals or even detect the crimes.

In the firewall security system, certain computers are dedicated to protecting valuable company information. They check all incoming and outgoing data, including the codes known only to authorized users.

Computer viruses

A computer virus is a tiny computer program that gets into a computer system along a telephone line or on a disk and causes trouble. It may make the whole system break down by telling the computer to remove, or wipe, its memory or data. There are hundreds of different viruses. Some are used secretly by business rivals to damage the computers of their competitors.

THE FUTURE OF COMPUTERS

A few keystrokes and you are on the "net"—the global Internet system of millions of computers linked by the wires and cables of the telecommunications system. Almost any information is at the user's fingertips, provided the telephone call can be paid for.

Computer models of the world economy predict that there will be little slowdown in the use and development of computers. Their processing power doubles and their costs halve about every eighteen months. New technologies are making chips and computers smaller and faster. They will find new uses in all kinds of industries.

The Information Revolution

About fifty million people worldwide are connected by the Internet, the international network of computers linked through the telecommunications system. They range from occasional users, exchanging information about their hobbies, to people who use it daily in their business.

The number of users may double in five years. This is the Information Revolution, when almost anyone will be able to dial into the Internet and get almost any information, from any source, anywhere in the world. Computers will be the vital tool in this electronic explosion. But already there are worries about secrecy and privacy. Who will control the immense electronic maze?

Artificial intelligence

Can computers ever be smarter than people? Perhaps. AI (Artificial Intelligence) is a huge research area for computing. However, it is more concerned with such things as the workings of the human brain, helping blind people to see, and making computer systems more effective and reliable, than in creating computer superbeings to rival humans.

In the future, computerized robots may help with the boring chores in our daily lives. But we probably would not want them to take over all the tasks we do.

Voice recognition

A major research aim is to make a computer that responds to the instructions of the human voice. The human brain manages voice recognition easily after millions of years of evolution. It is proving very difficult for the electronic brains of computers.

Slaves to computers

Can computers continue to become ever more important in daily life? Will people really want their lives to be based around a gray box, keyboard, and monitor? In the mid-1990s, computer games did not continue the rapid growth of previous years. Traditional toys, such as dolls and board games, made a dramatic comeback.

Perhaps people will react against the march of the computer. They might prefer to talk to real people instead of communicating with the use of monitors and cables. They may want to browse in real stores rather than go computer shopping in a store that exists only in cyberspace. They may want computers to remain as servants, rather than to become masters.

Computers are a part of daily life. But there is usually a limit to the time we want to spend sitting in front of these machines.

43

DATE CHART

1621 The slide rule is invented—a rulerlike device that uses logarithms (a form of mathematics) that enable the user to multiply and divide by adding or subtracting.

1642 Blaise Pascal invents the first practical mechanical calculator, which can add and subtract, using gears, levers, and cogs.

1832 Charles Babbage (left) devises the Analytical Engine, a sophisticated mechanical calculator programmed by a set of instructions on a punched card—but it is not built at the time.

1943 Alan Turing and his team develop Colossus, the first fully electronic calculating device, to crack enemy codes in World War II. But it is not fully programmable, so it is not a true computer.

1945 ENIAC, the Electronic Numerical Integrator and Computer (right), becomes the first machine that we would recognize as an electronic programmable computational device—a computer.

1948 The transistor is developed. It does a job similar to a vacuum tube, but uses much less electricity and is more reliable. At once, computer builders begin to make transistor-based computers, and sizes shrink by ten or a hundred times.

1951 UNIVAC 1 becomes the first electronic computer to go on sale as a commercial item, mainly for business use, and the first to store data on magnetic tape.

1956 FORTRAN is the first widely used high-level programming language, for the complicated arithmetic of engineering and science.

1965 Computer programming becomes accessible to the home user and hobbyist with the language BASIC (Beginner's All-purpose Symbolic Instruction Code).

1970 Floppy disks come into general use for storing data and programs.

1971 Intel introduces the first semiconductor microprocessor, or silicon chip, based on large-scale integration technology, as the main processing unit or heart of a computer. Its one silicon wafer replaces hundreds of transistors and other components.

1974 Hewlett Packard launches the first programmable pocket calculator, which can be programmed to do complex sums, but cannot handle words or graphics.

1975 The first kit-form personal computer, called the Altair 8800, goes on sale in the United States.

1977 The Apple II, the first widely successful, ready-built home computer, is introduced.

1979 The first spreadsheet programs (used mainly for handling numbers and for financial planning), developed by VisiCalc, become available to home computer users.

1981 IBM introduces its PC, using DOS, and sets standards for industry, office, and home computers that are still followed today.

1983 The Apple Macintosh computer is the first to use a mouse and pull-down menus (lists of options that appear on the screen, from which the user chooses an action).

1984 Some systems begin to use optical disks for storage of computer data, now known as CD-ROMs.

1986 Compaq introduces the first PCs to use 32-bit central processor chips, in advance of IBM.

1988 Computer parallel processing takes a leap forward with new programming methods that increase its speed by up to one thousand times.

1990s Microsoft introduces its Windows system of pull-down menus for IBM PCs, similar to the Apple Macintosh.

1993 "Multimedia" computers with enhanced graphics, stereo sound, interactive programs, and CD-ROM drives begin to sell in large numbers.

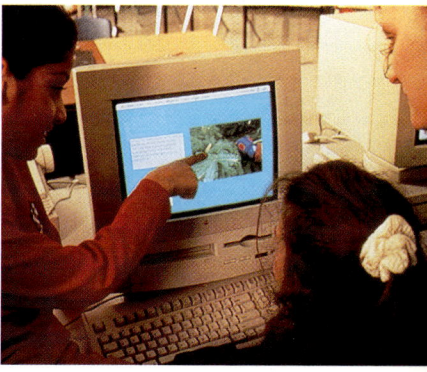

1995 Disney produces *Toy Story*, the world's first full-length animated movie made entirely by computers.

1995 Computer game machines enter a new era with the launch of the Sega Saturn and Sony Playstation.

GLOSSARY

air traffic control An organization that watches the flights of airplanes on radar screens and gives instructions to pilots by radio.

CD-ROM Compact Disc-Read Only Memory. A thin, hand-sized, plastic disk. It carries data in the form of patterns of tiny pits, detected by a laser beam. Information can be obtained from it, but the information on it cannot be changed.

circuit Paths that an electric current can flow through, including wires, transistors, and other devices. Printed circuits are formed when a thin coating is spread in a certain pattern on a surface.

database Data or information, such as a list of names and addresses and telephone numbers, stored in an organized way.

disk A thin, circular object where information can be stored in the form of coded patterns. Small magnetic disks in a protective case and designed mainly for transportation are called floppy disks. Larger disks inside the computer itself are called hard disks and can hold large amounts of data. CDs (Compact Discs) have a pattern of tiny pits read by a laser-beam head.

disk drive The device a disk is put into that can read or get information from the disk and write information onto the disk (unless the disk is ROM).

electronic Using very tiny pulses of electricity and with no obvious moving parts, unlike the switches, relays, and other moving parts of electrical or electro-mechanical systems.

fiber-optic cables Cables made of fibers of glass, along which information is sent as pulses of light.

keyboard A device with keys for inputting letters, numbers, and other data.

lasers (Light Amplification by Stimulated Emission of Radiation) Devices that produce an intense, narrow beam of pure light.

loaded When a program is transferred into the computer's memory.

magnetic disk see **disk**

magnetic tape Tape on which information can be stored in the form of coded magnetized patterns.

miniaturized Made or constructed on a very small scale.

mouse A computer input device that translates its movements, rolling across a surface, into the movements of an arrow or pointer on the computer screen. So called because it is roughly mouse-sized and has a "tail" wire that links it to the computer.

network Computers linked by cables or via modems and telephone lines, which work together.

orbit The path followed by a satellite in its motion around the earth.

printed circuits see **circuit**

read To get information, such as from a memory device (*see also* write).

stroboscopes Instruments that produce intense, flashing lights.

telecommunications network The system of interconnected devices—radio, television, telephone, etc.—that transmit information over a distance.

terminal Part of a computer system for getting data in and out, usually consisting of a keyboard and monitor, connected to the main computer.

volts Units used in measuring the force of electricity.

write To record information, such as in a memory device (*see also* read).

FIND OUT MORE

Books to read

Appleman, Dan. *How Computer Programming Works*. New York: Ziff-Davis, 1994.
The Computer Age. Understanding Science and Nature. Alexandria, VA: Time-Life Books, 1992.
Lambert, Mark. *Information Technology*. Technology in Action. New York: Bookwright Press, 1991.
White, Ron. How Computers Work. New York: Ziff-Davis, 1993.

Museums

Franklin Institute Science Museum and Planetarium
20th and Benjamin Franklin Parkway
Philadelphia, PA 19103
(215) 224-1200

National Inventors Hall of Fame
Inventure Place
221 South Broadway
Akron, OH 44208
(216) 451-0006

INDEX

Numbers in **bold** refer to illustrations

air traffic control 36–37, **36**
analog 17
art and design 30–33, **30**, **31**, **32**, **33**
ASCII codes 11

Babbage, Charles 6, **6**, 44
binary numbers 10, 11, 15, 17
business 4, 5, 8, 9, 34–35, 40–41, 42

computer modeling 38, 39
computer types
   laptops **5**
   mainframes 8
   microcomputers 9
   minicomputers 8
   palmtops **15**
   PCs 9, 10, 16, 19, 26, 39
crime 40–41

data 5, 7, 11, 12, 16, 44
database 14
desktop publishing **5**
digital 16, 17, 33

education 4, 5, 26–27, **26**, **27**
ENIAC 7, **7**, **8**, 44

films 4, 22–23, **22**, **23**, 45
first computers 6–7, **6**, **7**, 44

games 4, 5, 14, 16, 20–21, **20**, 24, 25, 27, 28, 40, 43, 45

hardware 12–13, **12**, **13**, 40
   clocks 13
   I/O cards 13
   PCBs 13
   (*see also* silicon chips)
   transformers 13
home 4, 9

input devices 16–17, **17**, 24
   cameras 17, 33
   CD-ROMs 14, 16, **16**, 27, 45
   disks 16, 19, 44
   graphics tablets 17, 23, 31
   joysticks 16, 20, **21**
   keyboards 4, 7, 12, 13, 14, 16, 20, 25, 43
   microphones 17
   mouse 13, 16, 20, 31, 32
   scanners 16, 33, 39
integrated circuits 8, 9, **9**, 10, 13, **14**, 23, 37
Internet 26, 41, 42, **42**

lasers 25, 34

maps 38–39, **38**
memory 5, 12, 14, 33
   (*see also* silicon chips)
modems 19, 40

output devices 18–19, **19**, 24
   loudspeakers 19
   monitors 4, **4**, 12, 13, 14, 16, 17, 18, **18**, 19, 27, **29**, 31, **31**, **36**, **37**, 43

output devices (*continued*)
   printers 18, 19

programs 5, 6, 7, 12, 14–15, 16, 20, 21, 22, 30, 36, 37, 40, 41, 45
   applications 14, 15
   languages 15, 44
   operating systems 14, 15, 16

register 34, **34**
robots 18, 37, **37**, **43**

security 40–41, **41**
silicon chips 8, 9, **9**, **12**, **13**, 36, 42, 45
   CPU 12, 14
   RAM 12
   ROM 12, 14, 20, 25
simulators **21**, 28–29, **28**, **29**

telecommunications network 4, 19, 42
training 28–29, **28**, **29**
transistors 8, 9, 44

vacuum tubes 8, **8**, 44
VLSI technology 9
VR (virtual reality) 24–25, **24**, **25**, 28, 29, **29**

weather forecasts 4, 39

© Copyright 1996 Wayland (Publishers) Ltd.